Global Cities
SYDNEY

Paul Mason
photographs by Rob Bowden

Evans

Published by
Evans Brothers Limited,
Part of the Evans Publishing Group,
2A Portman Mansions
Chiltern Street
London WIU 6NR

First published 2007
© copyright Evans Brothers Limited 2007

British Library Cataloguing in Publication Data

Mason, Paul
Sydney - (Global Cities)
1. Sydney (N.S.W) – Juvenile literature
I. Title
99.4'107
ISBN-10: 0237531240
13-digit ISBN 978 0237531249

Designer: Robert Walster, Big Blu Design
Maps and graphics by Martin Darlinson
All photographs are by Rob Bowden, apart from p.17 (Paul
Mason), p.22 (© Tim Wimborne/Reuters/Corbis) and p.56 (Dawne
Fahey/EASI-images).

Series concept and project management EASI –
Educational Resourcing
(info@easi-er.co.uk)

Contents

Living in an urban world   8

The history of Sydney   12

The people of Sydney   16

Living in Sydney   24

Sydney's economy   32

Managing Sydney   38

Transport in Sydney   42

Culture, leisure and tourism   46

Sydney's environment   52

The Sydney of tomorrow   56

Glossary   58

Further information   59

Index   60

Living in an urban world

Some time in 2007, history was made. For the first time ever, the world's population became more urban than rural. An estimated 3.3 billion people are now living in towns and cities like Sydney and, for many, urban living is fairly new. In China, for example, the number of people living in urban areas has grown from 196 million in 1980 to over 536 million by 2005.

The urban challenge...

This staggering rate of urbanisation (the process by which a country's population becomes concentrated in towns and cities) is being repeated across much of the world and presents us with a complex set of challenges for the twenty-first century. Many challenges are local: providing clean water for the people of expanding cities,

for example. Other challenges are global in scale. In 2003, an outbreak of the highly contagious SARS virus demonstrated this as it spread rapidly among the populations of cities across the globe. Pollution created by urban areas is also a concern, especially as urban residents tend to generate more pollution than their rural counterparts.

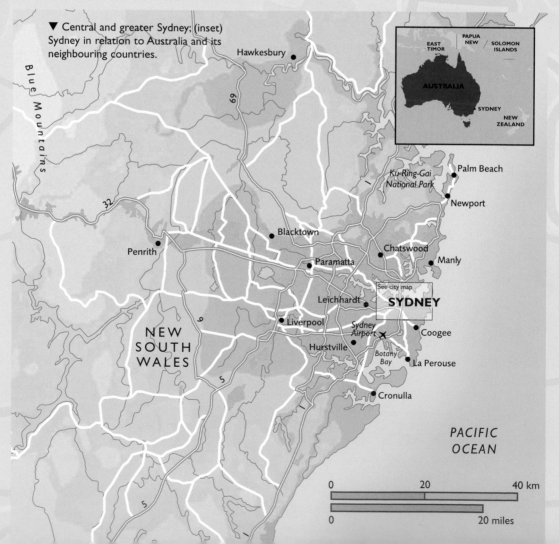

▼ Central and greater Sydney; (inset) Sydney in relation to Australia and its neighbouring countries.

... and opportunity!

Urban centres, particularly major cities like Sydney, also provide great opportunities for improving life. Cities concentrate people and allow for more efficient forms of mass transport, such as subway or light rail networks. Services such as waste collection, recycling, education and health care can all work more efficiently in a city. Cities are centres of learning, and often the birthplace of new ideas. They provide a platform for the celebration of arts and culture and as their populations become more multicultural, these become increasingly global in their reach.

▼ The central business district (CBD) of Sydney with the Royal Botanic Gardens and Sydney Opera House.

A global city

Although all urban centres will share certain features in common, in some cities the challenges and opportunities facing an urban world are particularly condensed. These are the world's global cities: they reflect the challenges of urbanisation, of globalisation, of citizenship and of sustainable development that face us all. Sydney is one of these global cities. The state capital of New South Wales with a powerful economy and vibrant culture, it is arguably the most important city in Australia and one of the most influential on the western Pacific rim, which stretches from the eastern coast of Australia in the south to China in the north. In Sydney, the challenges and opportunities of our urban future are being faced today.

The heart of the city

The heart of Sydney is the 'City of Sydney' area. Measuring just 26.15 sq km, the City lies on the south side of Sydney Harbour. The City has an importance far greater than its relatively tiny size suggests: this is where many international companies are based, in particular the financial services and telecommunications companies that are a significant part of the economy.

The historic centre of Sydney, the City is also the area that most tourist visitors head for. This is where they find attractions like the Royal Botanic Gardens, The Rocks (one of the oldest parts of Sydney), the modern-day fun of Darling Harbour, Chinatown and Sydney's most famous tourist destinations – the Opera House and Harbour Bridge. Tourism plays an important part in the city's economy, and the tourist attractions of the City help fill restaurants and hotel rooms across Sydney.

Less influential today than in the past is the City's industry sector. Although there

▲ At Sydney's centre lies the Central Business District, tightly packed with the offices of local and international businesses.

are still traditional industries, such as metal processing, in and around Sydney, they take up decreasing amounts of space and employ fewer people than in the past.

▲ The City of Sydney and metropolitan or greater Sydney.

Legend
- Motorway
- Main road
- Major rail
- Park

10

Metropolitan Sydney

Sydney has now spread out far beyond the edges of the City, the area where Sydney was founded. As Sydney got bigger, it began to swallow up the surrounding settlements, and these have now become part of metropolitan or 'greater' Sydney. Today, the area outside the City has 38 separate local government areas. These parts of Sydney's metropolitan area are generally known as the 'suburbs'.

▲ Manly is one of the largest suburbs of northern Sydney. The business district of central Sydney can be seen in the distance across the harbour.

The spreading city

Sydney's suburbs have spread north and south of the harbour, as well as inland. Today they reach inland almost to the foot of the Blue Mountains, the line of hills that begins 65km from the coast. The suburbs north and south of the harbour tend to hug the coastline, and have not spread anything like as far inland. Those north of the harbour are known as the northern-beach suburbs; those to the south are the southern-beach suburbs.

▲ Sydney has a very cosmopolitan population with people from a wide variety of ethnic backgrounds.

International mix of citizens

Sydney has citizens from a wide variety of international backgrounds. Australia as a whole has a long history of immigrant people arriving and settling into the Australian lifestyle – immigration is one of the things that makes Sydney a 'global' city. Today, most people are still descended from British immigrants, but there are also many others whose families came from mainland Europe, the Middle East, Asia and elsewhere living in Sydney.

The history of Sydney

Sydney is Australia's oldest city. The capital of the old British colony of New South Wales, it was established in 1788 with the arrival of the 'First Fleet' from England. The fleet was made up of 11 ships, carrying 1,030 people. Of these, 736 were criminals, part of whose sentence was to be sent overseas or 'transported'. Most of the rest were soldiers, brought to supervise the convicts.

The new colony

Early life in the colony was hard. The convicts were still serving their punishment and were forced to work to build the new settlement. Even for the soldiers and officials, sickness and starvation were very real threats. Until crops could be grown, the settlement was dependent on food supplied by sea from Europe. If one of the supply ships had failed to arrive, starvation could have followed for the whole colony.

Indigenous Australians

When the First Fleet arrived, they were far from being the first people to settle in Australia. Indigenous Australians (sometimes called Aborigines) had been living there for at least 40,000 years, probably longer, and had established thriving communities in areas such as Sydney. The British settlers ignored this; instead, the country was declared 'terra nullius', or land belonging to no one.

▲ William Bligh (1754-1817) was one of the first officers to hold any authority in Sydney and is credited with bringing order to the early city.

◄ Cadman's Cottage still stands on the site of the first buildings to have been built by English settlers around Sydney Cove (now Circular Quay).

This made it easier for the settlers to claim the land for England.

The area around Sydney Harbour was already part of the territory of the Cadigal band of the indigenous Eora people. The Eora, like Indigenous Australians elsewhere, soon began to fall victim to the European arrivals. They had no resistance to diseases like influenza and smallpox brought to Australia by the settlers. Over half the local population of Indigenous Australians was wiped out in a smallpox epidemic in 1789. Some indigenous people were driven from the land, or deliberately killed. Any who fought back were severely punished. Nonetheless, many did: among them was the resistance leader Pemulwuy, who became a figure of fear for many settlers until he was shot dead in 1802. One settler remembered:

"[Pemulwuy] or some of his party, were not idle about Sydney; they even ventured to appear within half a mile of the brickfield huts, and wound a convict who was going to a neighbouring farm on business. As one of our most frequent walks from the town was in that direction, this circumstance was rather unpleasant; but the natives were not seen there again."
(David Collins, *An Account of the English Colony in New South Wales, 1798*)

Today, there are tens of thousands of Indigenous Australians living in Sydney. They still find life tough, just as they do elsewhere in their country. Indigenous Australians have a lower life expectancy, worse health and education, and higher unemployment than any other Australians (see p.22-23).

▼ The Eora people suffered great hardships as a result of the colonisation of Sydney. Elements of their culture such as art and music (here artists play didgeridoos) are today important tourist attractions, but the Eora remain disadvantaged.

Sydney becomes a city

The population of Sydney continued to grow steadily over the years, boosted by the arrival of 'free' immigrants by the 1820s. The city was formally established in 1842, just after transportation to the state of New South Wales was halted by the British government. By this time Sydney was already becoming an important administrative and trading centre. Its earliest industries included the export of wool and wool products, sealing and whaling.

The great gold rush

In 1851, a prospector made Australia's first significant gold discovery in New South Wales. Within months, tens of thousands of hopeful people headed for the gold fields to make their fortune. Ships from Europe and North America became stranded in the harbour, after their crews deserted to go prospecting. The gold rush helped Sydney's population treble in less than 20 years and brought the first of what would become a significant Chinese population to the city.

▲ The General Post Office (GPO) building in the city centre is one of Sydney's many impressive Victorian public buildings.

Economic development

At the same time as the gold rushes were swelling Australian coffers, the Industrial Revolution was beginning in Britain. The factories of what most Australians still thought of as the 'old country', England, developed a ravenous hunger for raw materials: iron ore, wool, and other materials. Australia had these goods in abundance, and many of them were shipped back to Britain through the port of Sydney. As a consequence, the city grew rapidly in population and wealth. Many of Sydney's most impressive public buildings, such as the General Post Office, Town Hall and Australian Museum date from this prosperous time in the city's history.

▲ The Sydney Harbour Bridge is one of the world's most recognisable structures and provides a vital connection between the north and south of the city.

The twentieth century

By 1901, Sydney had half a million inhabitants and was one of the largest cities in the world. Although its population and industry continued to grow during the early twentieth century, the Great Depression of the 1930s hit Sydney hard, with many people out of work and 'swagmen' – homeless travelling men who slept rough – a common sight. One of the great accomplishments of the Depression era was the completion of the Sydney Harbour Bridge in 1932.

As the economy began to recover, suburbs like Pyrmont, Glebe and Redfern began to expand. Housing was cheap and there was plenty of work in nearby factories. During World War Two, Sydney was a base for the Allied forces in the Pacific, which brought large numbers of Americans to the city for the first time.

Recent development

Large areas of inner Sydney have recently undergone significant change and redevelopment. Factories, warehouses and

▲ Glebe is one of the more popular early suburbs located just outside the city centre. Many of its properties are now being renovated.

former workers' dwellings have been renovated and converted or replaced with office buildings, hotels, public buildings and apartments. The city has changed from an industrial centre to a growing residential and service-based employment centre. At the same time, Sydney's port has played a role of decreasing importance in the city's economy.

Sydney has become an extremely popular place to live. Since the 1990s the number of people living within the City has increased dramatically. The population of the City grew by 26.5 per cent between 1996 and 2001, while Sydney's population overall grew by 6.5 per cent.

The people of Sydney

Sydney today is home to people whose families came to Australia from all round the world. Over 70 per cent of 'Sydneysiders' (residents of Sydney) are a combination of two or more ethnic backgrounds and over 30 per cent were born overseas. As well as immigrants from Britain and mainland Europe, there are also significant communities from Southeast Asia, New Zealand and the Middle East.

▲ Today, people from many different ethnic origins are proud to call themselves Australians.

European city

Fifty years ago, Sydney was mostly a white, European city. The main reason for this was what became known as the 'White Australia' policy. Successive Australian governments wanted their country to remain European, and essentially British, in character. As politician (later Prime Minister) Alfred Deakin said in 1901:

"The unity of Australia is nothing, if that does not imply a united race. A united race not only means that its members can intermix, intermarry and associate without degradation on either side, but implies one inspired by the same ideas..." (Commonwealth Parliamentary Debates, 12 September 1901.)

Underpinning Deakin's statement was the idea that non-whites were inferior, and that if more were allowed into the country it would be 'degraded'.

Until the 1960s and 1970s, Sydney, like many Australian cities, was influenced by Britain and the USA. People's clothes, the cars they drove, the houses they lived in and the music they listened to would all have been familiar to a visitor from Britain or North America. After the Second World War, when US troops were stationed in Sydney and political ties between the USA and Australia grew stronger, American popular culture became increasingly important to young Australians and US music, cars, clothes, hairstyles and political views became more and more popular.

▲ American cars such as these old Chevrolets became popular in Sydney during the 1960s.

New openness

American influence wasn't confined to young people. Australian politicians also tended to support US policies, including sending troops to fight in America's war in Vietnam (which lasted from 1959 to 1975). This war became increasingly unpopular in Australia, and by the 1970s demonstrations against it were common in Sydney and other cities.

In 1972, moved partly by unhappiness about the war in Vietnam, Australians elected a new government, led by Gough Whitlam. Whitlam quickly brought the troops home and ended conscription. Also, the 'White Australia' policy was effectively ended by his radical policies, which made it easier for non-English speakers to make a new life in Australia.

CASE STUDY

James Tarbet, UK immigrant to Sydney

James moved to Sydney to work in the medical publishing industry. He settled in the Surry Hills district and, having planned only to stay a couple of years, is still living in the city five years later.

"I think one of the reasons Sydney is so popular with Europeans, especially English people, is that it feels very fresh and new – there aren't many European cities where you get woken up by flocks of parrots outside your window in the morning, and the different cultures here make the city an interesting place to live. But at the same time, it's quite familiar: everyone speaks English, you can get familiar food if you want it, and there's a friendliness that makes it an easier place to live than, say, New York, where I had worked previously."

The Asia-Pacific Rim

Further changes in political outlook came to Australia and Sydney in particular from the 1980s, as immigrants from Southeast Asia and China began to arrive in increasing numbers, many settling in Sydney. Prime Minister Paul Keating (in power from 1991) encouraged Australians to see themselves as part of the Asia-Pacific Rim, rather than as an outpost of Europe. Keating also campaigned to abandon having the British monarch as head of state, urging Australians to cut their ties to Britain, but this proposal was defeated in a referendum in 1999.

▶ Chinatown is the most obvious symbol of Asian immigration to Sydney, but people from the Asia-Pacific region are today integral to many aspects of city life.

Changing population

Today, Sydney is a very different place from the ethnically homogenous city of the 1950s. A few statistics reveal how Sydney has changed from the mostly white, mostly English-speaking city it used to be. The metropolitan area now has a population of 4.4 million, as compared to a population of 1.7 million in 1950. Half of the City of Sydney's residents were born overseas, many in Asian Pacific countries, and 30 per cent of these residents speak a language other than English as their first language.

Half of the City of Sydney residents are also between 20 and 40 years old, making

▼ Metropolitan Sydney has expanded to cover a vast area of 12,145 sq km.

the inner core of Sydney a very 'young' city. The average age of residents increases in the suburbs, as many people move there when they have children, drawn by the larger houses, with gardens and possibly a swimming pool. Even so, Sydney's expansion through immigration has kept the average age of its citizens low. Another factor in this is that older Sydneysiders have previously chosen to retire to smaller communities outside the city.

▶ Passing the time of day in Darling Harbour. The city centre has a particularly youthful population of young working professionals and students.

CASE STUDY

Aur Jong Sun, Korean immigrant to Sydney

Aur Jong Sun, known to his friends as Johnny, is from South Korea. After studying and completing his military service in South Korea, Johnny decided to move overseas and came to Sydney in 2004. "I am studying at the moment, especially to improve my language. If I want to live here then I must speak English. I like Sydney and the people here – they are very open-minded and you are free to be yourself. People mix very well and there are lots of other Koreans here to show you around. I like all of the green space too. You are never far from some open space and I like the outdoor life and sports. Here I can do exercise whenever I want. I played my first game of soccer on real grass here! I would like to settle in Sydney and work in advertising. If I had to go back to Korea now I would miss the friendly people and their smiles. And the beach!"

◀ Aur Jong Sun is studying to improve his English in Sydney.

A diverse city

Sydney is home to many different communities. Immigrants traditionally settle in cities, where they are most likely to find work, housing and people who speak their mother tongue. Sydney's position as Australia's wealthiest city has drawn immigrants from all round the world.

▲ A group of Italian Sydneysiders enjoy a game of lawn bowls in Waverley, one of the many suburbs in which there is an Italian presence.

The first immigrants were British and Irish, who made up 80 per cent of the immigrant community in 1901. In the twentieth century things changed rapidly: by 1954, only just over half of immigrants came from the British Isles. Another third came from elsewhere in Europe, mainly from Italy, Greece, Germany, the Netherlands and Poland. By 2002, partly thanks to Australia's new immigration policies, 15 per cent of immigrant Australians came from Asian or Pacific countries such as China, Vietnam, the Philippines, India, Malaysia and Sri Lanka. In 1954, people from these countries had made up just two per cent of immigrant Australians. Each of these groups has their own community in Sydney, existing within the larger community of Sydneysiders. The city's restaurants, shops, festivals and languages all reflect Sydney's diversity.

Conflicts

Occasionally there have been conflicts between Sydney's different ethnic groups. During the early twenty-first century, these conflicts focused on Muslim immigrants. In 2002, a bomb planted by Muslim terrorists in Bali killed 89 Australians. Anger at these deaths added to existing tensions with Lebanese Muslim citizens.

Tensions on the beaches

In 2005, fights broke out between groups of white Australian youths and members of other ethnic groups. The conflict began when two beach lifeguards were beaten up by a group of Lebanese youths from the western suburbs. The Sunday after the attack on the lifeguards, several thousand protesters gathered under a 'Reclaim The Beach' banner: among their slogans were, 'We Grew Here, You Flew Here'. Police reacted in large numbers, and the protests were quickly stopped. Nonetheless, low-level hostility between the Lebanese of the western suburbs and European Australians of the beach suburbs continues.

▼ Sydney's beaches have been the scene of recent ethnic tensions.

The suburbs and the City

Housing is generally cheapest and therefore most available to new immigrants, who often arrive in Australia hoping to make a better life for themselves, furthest from the City of Sydney. The western, inland suburbs in particular provide inexpensive housing for immigrant families. Some immigrant populations have tended to settle in particular areas of Sydney, giving them a distinct cultural identity. The suburb of Marrickville has a large Greek population, for example, while Cabramatta is home to many Vietnamese and Chinese immigrants.

The City of Sydney is home to a variety of different ethnic groups. Nearly 30 per cent of residents speak a language other than English. Some notable areas in the City include Chinatown and Indigenous Australian communities.

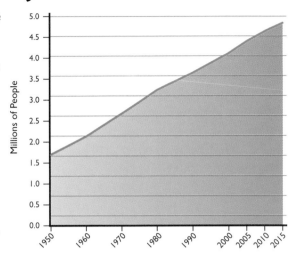

▲ This graph shows the steep growth in Sydney's population since 1950, and projects its increase up to 2015. Immigration has contributed greatly to Sydney's expansion.

▼ Sydney's Chinese community enjoys celebrations as part of Chinese New Year. Sydney's Chinese New Year celebrations are some of the biggest outside of China.

Indigenous Australians

'Indigenous Australians' refers to Aborigines and islanders from the Torres Straits, north of the mainland. Those who live in Sydney are mainly Aborigines. More Indigenous Australians live in western Sydney than anywhere else in Australia. There are also big communities in the City, the best known being in Redfern. Indigenous Australians have a lower standard of living than any other group in Australia.

In terms of health, Indigenous Australians are ten times more likely to suffer from diabetes than other Australians and seven times more likely to die of respiratory disease. Infant mortality is between two and three times as high as for other Australians. Overall, their life expectancy is 16 to 18 years lower.

When it comes to employment, Indigenous Australians are similarly disadvantaged. Their unemployment rate is three times as high as the national average. They also earn roughly two thirds as much as their non-indigenous counterparts. Moreover, Indigenous Australians are more likely to live in overcrowded housing (over 30 per cent do, against an overall average of eight per cent), and are less likely to own their own home (27 per cent compared to a national average of 69 per cent).

Many Indigenous Australians live in Sydney, and these statistics provide a guide to what their lives are like. Unsurprisingly, perhaps, indigenous communities have sometimes clashed with the authorities.

Of course, not all Indigenous Australians live the lives of deprivation suggested by national statistics. Many Indigenous Australians have forged successful careers, becoming judges, professors, doctors and lawyers. Professor Larisa Behrendt, for example, won a scholarship to study law at Harvard University in the USA, and now teaches law and indigenous studies at Sydney's University of Technology. Indigenous Australians have also excelled in theatre, film and sports. One of the most famous Australian athletes is Cathy Freeman, who won a gold medal in the 400m race at the 2000 Sydney Olympics.

▼ A local resident sweeps up broken glass in the wake of violent clashes between police and Indigenous Australians in Redfern in February 2004.

Indigenous Australian initiatives

The Indigenous Australian community has come up with a number of initiatives to help improve the lives of Indigenous Australians living in Sydney. These are concerned mainly with improving people's health care, housing and education. Other initiatives aim to help Indigenous Australians whose lives are being ruined by drink or drugs.

Some initiatives look to give young Indigenous Australians specific opportunities. One of the most interesting of these is 'Lights Camera Action!', which is based in the Redfern Community Centre. This project gives young Indigenous Australians the chance to develop new skills, with the aim of being employed in film, television or theatre work. There is access to training courses, and 'Camera Action!' also acts as a talent agency. Young people register and have photos taken (paid for by the City government) which are added to a website that casting agents can use. The initiative has helped many young Indigenous Australian actors launch their careers in film, TV and advertising.

▼ This mural in the inner-city suburb of Woolloomooloo was designed and completed by local youths working with local Aboriginal artist, Danny Eastwood. It depicts the story of Sydney from the first inhabitants to the modern day and is an example of communities working together to share their cultures.

Living in Sydney

Most Sydneysiders have a high standard of living. The climate is generally excellent — warm and dry. People tend to live in well-built homes, in pleasant environments and with a good salary. These are some of the reasons why a 2005 survey decided that Sydney was the seventh best city in the world in which to live. (Three other Australian cities came ahead of Sydney, though: second best was Melbourne, fifth Perth and sixth Adelaide.)

Green spaces

One of the features which makes Sydney such an attractive city is its parkland. Urban planning and development have placed great importance on retaining the city's green spaces, such as the green areas behind Sydney's beaches, Hyde Park and Centennial Park. Even in the heart of the City, in amongst some of the most valuable land in Australia, there is space for the large Royal Botanic Gardens. Further out, in the suburbs, there are even areas of rural and agricultural land.

CASE STUDY

Pat Houlcroft, Coordinator of Botanic Horticulture at Sydney's Botanic Gardens

Pat Houlcroft's role is to manage a team of 12 workers in the day-to-day maintenance of the gardens. This is an enormous task and Pat explains that there are particular challenges caused by the gardens' attractiveness to wildlife.

▲ Foliage is stripped by the roosting flying foxes.

"The gardens are a refuge for wildlife in Sydney and biodiversity is very important, but wildlife can also cause problems. The best example is the grey-headed flying fox. They use the gardens to roost during the day, but this is causing damage to our trees as they destroy the upper canopy. The bats also create a mess with their faeces, which can be unpleasant for visitors. We have up to 10,000 flying foxes in the gardens and this is unsustainable. There are plans to use a sound deterrent to drive the flying foxes away. This worked in Melbourne and we need to protect this important green space for everyone."

City by the sea

The sea, or more accurately, the beach, is an important part of life for Sydney's people, as well as drawing many visitors to the city. The most famous beach of all is Bondi, but north and south of here there are plenty of other beaches. Many beaches have an area where there are public grills: 20 cents in a slot buys you a few minutes of cooking time. People bring their lunch and soon the grills are piled high. All the time, there are games of frisbee, swimming, surfing and other activities going on. It can get very busy, particularly at weekends, with people driving from far inland to spend a bit of time on the beach.

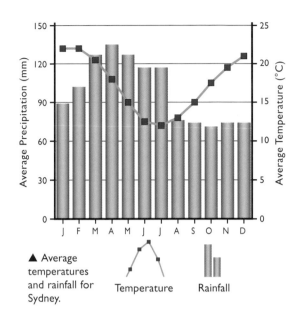

▲ Average temperatures and rainfall for Sydney.

Temperature   Rainfall

Inequalities

While the standard of living in Sydney is generally high, there are still areas of poverty. Salaries are higher in the City than in the metropolitan area in general: in 2004 they averaged US$433 a week, against a citywide average of US$334. Even within the City there are big inequalities: over a quarter of people earned over US$750 a week, but almost a fifth had a salary of less than US$250.

The inequalities of wealth between some citizens can lead to problems. There is a connection between poverty and alcohol and drug abuse and Sydney, like all major cities, suffers from crime related to these, such as burglary and mugging. There are also criminal gangs in the city controlling the drugs trade and prostitution, for example.

◀ Poverty can be found even in the heart of Sydney's prosperous business district. This homeless man is offering shoe polishing to try to earn some money.

Housing in Sydney

Sydney's population has grown enormously over the last 100 years – from just 500,000 inhabitants in 1900 to four and a half million in 2005 – and is forecast to continue to rise. The number of single people and child-free couples is also predicted to grow significantly in the years to come, and planners suggest that almost half a million new homes for single people or couples will be needed in Sydney by

▲ This block of 'units' (like flats) in Summer Hill is typical of the new multi-residency housing that Sydney will need in the future.

2020. Most of these will be for people in the under-30 and over-50 age groups.

In the past, Sydney's traditional answer to an increase in the population has been for the city to spread out, with new homes being built in the suburbs on the outskirts of the metropolitan area, away from the sea or harbour. Property here is generally cheaper than in the City. These new, suburban homes were typically 'family' houses with several bedrooms, a garden and garage. Such homes are less suitable for singles or couples, who need less space and generally prefer to be nearer the city centre. They also take a land-hungry approach to providing new housing, meaning that the once-green areas at the fringes of the city area have been built on more and more. The ever-increasing distance of new homes from the city centre has created growing levels of traffic, as people use their cars to get around.

Building for the future

Plans for the future aim to develop new homes in Sydney in a different way. More multi-occupancy homes are being built, such as apartment blocks with smaller areas of accommodation, suitable for singles and couples. Planners are taking care to include features such as lifts and ramps, which will help older people who are less able to move around easily. Homes are also being built on 'brownfield' sites – areas of land in the city that have previously been used for other activities.

As a result of population changes and these new building initiatives, the proportion of detached houses in the City has been steadily dropping over the last few years, from just under 70 per cent in 1991 to just over 60 per cent in 2001. At the same time, the proportion of semi-detached houses and flats has risen from just over 30 per cent to over 35 per cent.

▲ New apartments in the suburb of Mosman are an example of the high-density housing now becoming more evident in Sydney.

Building in the city centre

New homes are also much less likely to be built on the outskirts of Sydney than was the case until the turn of the century. In 1993/4, 68 per cent of new homes were built in the outer regions. By 2000/1, this percentage had gone down to 49 per cent. Over the same period, homes created in inner-city areas doubled from 13 per cent to 26 per cent. The overall effect of these changes is that Sydney's population is steadily being concentrated in the city's centre. This is a more sustainable situation, creating less pollution and threatening less of Sydney's valuable green outer areas.

▲ This new development in the centre of Sydney is being sold as a 'vertical village', comprising retail, office and accommodation space.

Shops and shopping

The structure of housing in Sydney affects the types of places where people shop for everyday essentials. In the suburbs, where there are greater distances between homes and workplaces, people's transport is more car-based. They are more likely to drive to shops, which therefore need to have space for parking but don't necessarily have to be near people's homes. In the City, more journeys are made on foot or using public transport: people buy smaller amounts of shopping, closer to home.

▲ The Queen Victoria Building is the most famous shopping arcade in Sydney and one of two Victorian arcades that survive today.

Food

Sydneysiders have a choice of fresh fruit, vegetables, meat and fish available to them that would be the envy of many cities in northern Europe or North America. Close by the city are the market gardens and fruit growers of the Blue Mountains, as well as a good supply of cattle, sheep and poultry. Sydney's fish market is crammed with fresh fish of all kinds.

▲ A juice bar in The Rocks area of Sydney. Sydney has a wealth of fresh produce and juice bars are a firm favourite during the hot summer months.

Nevertheless, Sydney's citizens suffer from the diet-related health problems that affect many city dwellers in wealthy countries, often as a result of eating too many ready meals and fast food. Most of these health problems are related to obesity, which is a growing problem. Australia has among the world's highest rates of diabetes, which is linked to obesity, and shares relatively high rates of heart disease with countries such as the UK and USA. These trends are reflected among the health problems of the people of Sydney.

◄ Cattle graze on farmland to the north of Sydney. The area around the city is a major food-producing region.

CASE STUDY

Steve Westaway (Tibby), auctioneer, Sydney Fish Market

Sydney Fish Market is the largest seafood market in the southern hemisphere. The market is not only one of the biggest in the world, but has the second greatest range of fresh, mainly Australian, seafood, with over 100 different species being sold on any single day. "We sell around 15,000 tonnes of seafood each year to fish retailers and restaurants," explains Tibby. "The public can buy from the retail markets here too. Most of the fish we sell is auctioned using a computerised Dutch, or 'reverse', auction system. Originally developed by the Dutch to sell flowers en masse, the starting price is set by an auctioneer higher than the regular market price; it then drops. The person to make the first bid 'wins' the purchase. The buyers sit at terminals and watch the auction price on the large clock-like displays. They press a button to stop at the price they are willing to pay and that is it – sold! It looks complicated, but is quite simple really. Some species such as the tuna, sharks, crabs and lobsters are

auctioned in the old fashioned way because buyers need to inspect them closely for quality. This is more pressure on us, but it is still enjoyable to be in the thick of it."

▼ The computerised Dutch auction system.

Education

In Australia, the state governments run education. In Sydney this means that the schools are the responsibility of the New South Wales government. Children go to primary, secondary and post-secondary schools and colleges. Most start pre-school at three, though they do not have to attend until they are six. Compulsory schooling ends at the age of 16.

Parents can choose to send their children to state or private schools. At both students usually have to wear a uniform. State schools are in theory free, though many schools do ask parents to pay a small amount towards the cost of their children's education. The private schools are more expensive. Among the private schools in Sydney is the oldest school in Australia, King's School, which first opened in 1831.

Education is not confined to school, with children continuing to learn at after-school clubs and sports groups. One of the most popular of these is the 'Little Nippers' surf lifesaving club, where children can learn about ocean safety and lifesaving.

Post-secondary education

After leaving school at 16, young Australians can start post-secondary education. This usually involves either a one or two-year vocational training course at an institute of technical and further education, or a three or four-year degree course at a state university. Sydney is home to the University of New South Wales, the University of Sydney, the University of Technology, the University of Western Sydney and the Sydney campus of the Australian Catholic University. These five alone enrol well over 100,000 students a year, and there are many other post-secondary educational organisations in the city. This high level of education helps Australia compete with other leading world economies.

◀ The University of Sydney is one of the most prestigious universities in Australia.

Adult education

One in five adult Australians struggles to read easily. For them, and for people who want to learn other new skills, there is a range of adult-education opportunities available in Sydney. These include the chance for new immigrants to the city to improve their skills in English at specialist colleges. Learning English is a key skill for new immigrants, as it allows them to understand and take a full part in the life of their new country. It also helps them to find work more easily.

CASE STUDY

Noh Hyun Jun, Korean English language student

Noh Hyun Jun is a student at the University of Technology in Sydney. He came to the university from South Korea and is hoping to gain qualifications to work in environmental engineering. "I was a high school teacher in Korea with interest in environmental issues and biology. I came to Sydney because I want to study about the environment and Australians are more environmentally aware than back home. I would like to study a Masters course in Environmental Engineering here at UTS and then get a job working for the government. This year I am concentrating on learning English though. The education system is very good here and there are people from many different countries. I am learning so much and really hope I can continue my studies in Sydney."

Health care

The costs of health care are divided between the state government and the federal government, with the New South Wales State government taking most of the responsibility for Sydney's health care services. These include:
- Hospitals
- Community and school health centres
- Maternal and child health care centres
- Residential care homes for the elderly
- Dental services.

Everyone is entitled to free health care at public hospitals through the federal Medicare scheme. If they go to see a doctor at a local surgery, Medicare pays 85 per cent of the cost. However, many Sydneysiders who can afford it have private health insurance. They pay a monthly or annual amount in return for knowing that their medical costs will be covered if they fall ill or have an accident.

Sydney's economy

The economy of the City of Sydney alone had a value of about US$47 billion in 2003/4. To put this giant number in context, it represents over eight per cent of Australia's total economy. If the entire metropolitan area is included, the value of the economy is three times the size. Sydney dominates Australia's international business scene: the city is the Australian headquarters of many foreign companies, and two thirds of international business visitors are heading for Sydney.

▲ The central business district is the hub of the Sydney economy and home to many international companies.

Modern economy

The outer areas of Sydney have retained more of the city's traditional industrial activities, particularly metal processing and sheet metal industries, than the centre. They are also home to most of the city's newer manufacturing jobs, such as manufacturing of defence industry materials and car parts. More important for the city centre are service industries. These include computer-based industries such as banking and telecommunications, plus the retail

◄ Banks and telecom companies are clustered in north Sydney, just across the harbour bridge.

trade and tourism. In 2004, 2.4 million international visitors came to Sydney, plus many more from within Australia, helping to create jobs in related industries such as the restaurant business, transport and retail.

The growth industries in Sydney during the twenty-first century are forecast to be in two areas. The first is information-based activities such as telecommunications, banking and financial services. The second is people-serving industries, such as the retail trade, tourism, caring for the elderly, health care and personal services.

▲ The busy trading floor at Macquarie Bank in Sydney.

CASE STUDY

Doug Webber, Associate Director at Macquarie Bank

Doug Webber is an Associate Director of the Financial Services Group at Macquarie Bank in Sydney, one of the largest financial service providers in Australia. Founded in 1969, Macquarie Bank has grown from its Sydney base to operate offices in 23 countries and with a global staff of around 8,200, 2,517 of them overseas. Sydney remains core to the company however, as Doug explains: "Sydney is the main financial centre in Australia and one of the most important centres in the world. It is a good location, particularly for the growing Asian markets, right on our doorstep and in similar time zones. These markets will be a strong focus over the next 20 years or so. Sydney has grown as a financial centre since the deregulation of the banking sector in 1984. This combined with the incredible changes in technology have allowed the sector to grow enormously. There are now many international banks

with a base in Sydney; it is an attractive place to do business. Macquarie remains a strong company thanks to its history of innovation in offering new financial services. We call it financial engineering. This innovation comes partly from a mentality of self sufficiency that is strong in Sydney and has been since the first settlers came here."

Industry and manufacturing

The level of industrial and manufacturing employment in Sydney has changed significantly in recent decades. Sydney's traditional economic activity was related to its use as a port and a processing centre for raw materials, ranging from wool to coal and metal.

Industries that were once important, such as metalworking, mining and clothing manufacture, still exist in modern-day Sydney. However, they employ an increasingly small proportion of Sydney's people. Mechanisation and globalisation, in the form of competition from nearby Asian markets where labour costs are lower, have had a negative effect on these businesses. Today, the heartland of Sydney's manufacturing is in the outer areas. Even here, though, experts forecast a decline in the number of manufacturing jobs in all but three of Sydney's 19 economic zones. What manufacturing there is in Sydney is extremely varied. It ranges from high-tech industries, food processing and timber products to engineering, defence industries and the production of car parts.

CASE STUDY

John Boyle, metalworker

John Boyle works at Central Foundry in Mascot, a family business managed by John's father, Kevin. They make non-ferrous metal castings that range from decorative lattice work for houses, to urban street furniture such as bus stops and smart poles used for city surveillance. They also specialise in making yacht keels. As markets become more global, John's family have seen many manufacturing businesses close, but John's father Kevin explains how they keep going: "There is a lot of competition from Asia and especially China, but the key to our success is quality and after-sale support. Keeping pace with changes is constant though. We have invested in automated technology and follow tight environmental standards to protect both the environment and our workers. We have waterless processes for example, and our

gas-fired furnaces have low emissions. People care about these things today. The challenges for the future are more about skills than anything. It is hard to find young people who want to work in manufacturing and the skills are slowly dying out. The government helps to fund apprenticeships and the like, but people have got to want to do it too!"

Regeneration and redevelopment

As traditional industries declined in the centre of Sydney, some of the areas they had traditionally occupied fell into disuse and became derelict. The city's government realised that these old industrial regions needed to be given a new function and have taken action to redevelop the land for warehousing, shopping facilities, housing or visitor attractions. The City is currently planning redevelopments of some of its run-down former industrial areas. Among those earmarked are the old Carlton and United Brewery, and Green Square.

The old Carlton and United Brewery closed in 2003. It is in Chippendale, an area on the edge of Sydney's Central Business District and the city has targeted the site for

▲ Derelict business premises earmarked for redevelopment as part of the Green Square urban renewal project.

redevelopment as 'an environmentally sustainable mixed-use development'. It is hoped that the old brewery site will one day become the location of businesses and homes, with public areas featuring art displays, walking and cycling routes to the surrounding areas, as well as a child-care facility.

Green Square will be the largest urban renewal project in Australia, and aims to bring new life to an area of 2.78 sq km of land between the CBD and Port Botany to the south.

◀ The new station at Green Square provides high-speed transfer to both the airport and the city centre. It will become the core of the redeveloped region.

Darling Harbour and The Rocks

Examples of what can happen when old industrial areas are redeveloped can be found at Darling Harbour and The Rocks, both of which have undergone the kind of transformation planned for areas like the Carlton and United Brewery.

Sydney's first citizens called Darling Harbour 'Cockle Bay', because of the large numbers of shellfish that could be found there. Later it became the city's main industrial area, with docks, a railway yard and an international shipping terminal. By the 1980s, however, Darling Harbour had fallen on hard times, due largely to its decline as a port, and the Sydney Harbour Foreshore Authority was formed to redevelop the area.

By 1988, in time for the 200th anniversary of the first settlers reaching Australia, the work was complete. Today Darling Harbour is home to a shopping centre, the Sydney Convention Centre, about 15 different hotels, over 100 restaurants and eateries, the Sydney Aquarium, National Maritime Museum and an IMAX theatre, among other attractions. Millions of people now visit Darling Harbour each year, spending large sums of money and demonstrating the transformation in part of Sydney's economy from the old industries to the new. An added advantage is that so many attractions all in one site have a far smaller, more sustainable impact on the city's environment than if they were spread out across the entire city.

▼ Part of the redevelopment at Darling Harbour.

Bob Deacon, General Manager of the Darling Harbour Complex

The Darling Harbour complex is a showcase of urban renewal and one of Sydney's main tourist attractions. "What you see here today" explains Bob, "was all old industrial land, disused and decaying. It was a real eyesore and a huge area of prime land right near the city centre. The Sydney Harbour Foreshore Authority has made it one of the best waterfronts in the world." Darling Harbour reopened in 1988 and today has almost 3,000 hotel rooms, more than 9,000 restaurant/café seats and Australia's premier conference centre. There are also

shopping and entertainment venues as well as specific attractions like the Sydney Aquarium and the Chinese Garden of Friendship. "Tourism is vital to Darling Harbour" says Bob, "and overseas visitors make up around 54 per cent of our visitors. Since 1988, more than 160 million people have visited the complex. Darling Harbour is also for the people of Sydney however, and Sydneysiders make up around a third of our visitors, coming twice a month on average. We host numerous special events throughout the year to encourage people to keep coming back. There is always something new for them to experience."

◀ Sydney Aquarium, Darling Harbour.

Another area that has been redeveloped from industrial use is The Rocks. This is where convict tents were first erected in 1788, but has now also been turned into a tourist attraction. Besides its historic streets and buildings, The Rocks also boasts shops, restaurants and an excellent street market every Sunday morning.

▶ The Rocks marks where the First Fleet settlers landed in Sydney in 1788.

Managing Sydney

Sydney does not have an overall governing body for the city. Instead, there are 38 separate local government areas. Their main responsibilities are for local infrastructure such as roads, libraries and refuse collection. The local governments work under the guidance of the federal and state governments, with the state government the major influence. The state government responsibilities are mostly in the areas of health, education, housing, transport and local law enforcement.

▼ The Town Hall is the seat of the City of Sydney council.

City and state

The City of Sydney does have its own mayor, as do other areas within the metropolitan area, but unlike many other global cities, Sydney does not have an overall leader, just as it doesn't have an overall city government. There are two main reasons for this:

First, Sydney wasn't always as big as it is now: as it spread, it has swallowed up smaller towns, which already had identities and governments they did not want to lose.

Second, if Sydney had its own government, it would be a rival to the New South Wales government. More people live in Sydney than the rest of the state. An

▲ Local councils and the City of Sydney take their own responsibility for aspects of urban management such as street cleaning.

elected government of the city would be in a powerful position to argue for the city's interests, which might not be the best thing for the state as a whole.

CASE STUDY

Clover Moore, MP, Lord Mayor of Sydney

"Australia's three-tier (federal, state and local) system of government presents challenges for managing Sydney. As Lord Mayor, I am the elected representative of central Sydney, but not of the whole metropolitan area.

Sydney is made up of 38 local councils that have responsibility in their own areas for land use planning and development, management of parks and gardens, library services, construction and maintenance of roads and footpaths, and waste management.

The NSW State Government is responsible for many issues that are local government responsibilities in other countries, such as public transport, policing and education.

The City of Sydney Council seeks to provide quality and innovative local services, while taking a leadership role on larger issues. Cooperation with adjacent councils and the state government is needed to implement larger cross border projects and achieve effective metropolitan-wide planning."

Community action

Sydneysiders often take a keen interest in the government of their city. They vote in the compulsory elections of course, but they also get involved in community action. One example of this was the way in which local residents helped steer the plans for the old Carlton and United Brewery (see page 35) in a direction that they thought would be best for the area. The residents' campaign was led by FOCUS (the Friends Of Carlton United Site).

▲ The Carlton and United brewery buildings close to Central Station. Community groups have been instrumental in determining the future development of the site.

There are many other community groups in Sydney. The City of Sydney website lists 19 resident associations, and the City is just one of nearly 40 different local government areas in metropolitan Sydney. The subjects covered at just one meeting between the City and resident groups for a single area, Surry Hills, give an idea of the wide variety of subjects that local citizens are involved in or concerned about:
  •New Surry Hills Library, childcare centre and neighbourhood centre
    •Belvoir Street Theatre
    •Frog Hollow Nature Reserve
    •New public toilets

▲ An alcohol-free-street policy is one of the many community actions to be implemented in the Surry Hills district.

  • Discarded syringes
  • Homelessness services
  • Traffic management.

As well as the resident associations, which are based in particular locations, some community groups are based around specific issues. One example of this is the campaign against a road-building and widening scheme for the Marrickville area, begun in 2005. Fear of the new road, which meant the demolition of homes and historical buildings, united people from a wide variety of backgrounds. Another example is Sydney's Meals On Wheels service, which uses volunteer drivers to deliver food to elderly people.

Wendi Balbi, volunteer (2000 Olympics and Taronga Zoo)

Wendi Balbi knows all about community involvement, having been one of the leading pioneer volunteers for the 2000 Olympic Games. Wendi was among some 560 pioneers who volunteered as far back as 1997 to help in the build up to the games, recruiting and training other volunteers and testing everything to make sure the games would pass without a hitch. She remembers the long days of preparation and hard work, but says it was worth every minute. "I can remember the growing tension and excitement and then suddenly the Games were upon us. I was working in the VIP lounge during the opening ceremonies and had a good view of this spectacular event, but the highlight of the day came later on the way home. Everyone was excitedly talking to all and sundry and the bus was alive with community singing at three o'clock in the morning. Sydney was transformed." The legacy of the games is still evident with a

strong volunteer ethic says Wendi. "Volunteering continues to play an important role in my life too. It brings its rewards in the form of friendships, knowledge, and a feeling that in some small way one is contributing to the community. At present my life-long love of birds has led me to volunteer at Taronga Zoo, bird watching. You never know where the next avenue will lead."

▼ Service medals awarded to Wendi as as Olympic volunteer.

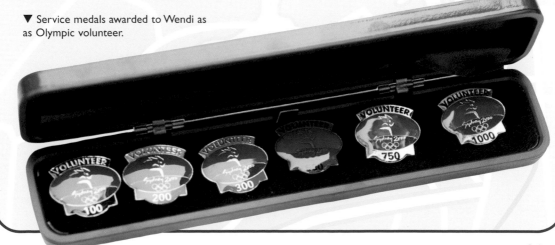

Transport in Sydney

Sydney has good transport links, with a combination of road, rail, ferry, cycle and pedestrian transport. The city's roads are often busy, however, and at rush hour getting even a short distance in a car or bus can take a long time.

Car culture

As Sydney expanded out into the suburbs during the second half of the twentieth century, increasing numbers of people found themselves living further away from the rail network. As a result, they became dependent on cars as a means of transport. This trend continued right up to the end of the century and beyond, and car use increased massively. Between 1981 and 2001, for example, the population increased by 21 per cent. At the same time, the number of journeys by car increased by 41 per cent, the actual number of cars by 58 per cent, and the number of kilometres travelled by car almost doubled.

▶ Commuters at Summer Hill station in the inner west of the city. Though the trains are well used, many commuters drive rather than use public transport.

Road congestion

Because of Sydney's spread-out nature, and the reliance on cars as a way of getting around, road congestion is an increasing problem. Main routes such as the Parramatta Road, Victoria Road and Military Road are regularly jammed. The basic problem is that most people live outside the central areas of Sydney, but their jobs are elsewhere, usually in the centre. Today, 70 per cent of journeys to work are made by car. During the morning and evening rush hours congestion is particularly bad, but the roads are only rarely free-flowing.

◀ Heavy traffic during the morning rush hour on Victoria Road, one of the main arterial roads in Sydney.

Congestion problems

Traffic congestion on the scale that happens in Sydney causes a number of serious problems. Businesses lose money because of congestion: people are late for work because of the traffic (from 1995 to 2005, the time it took Sydneysiders to get to work each day rose by seven per cent), and delivering goods takes extra time.

Large numbers of cars with their engines running, moving slowly through the streets, emit a lot of air pollution (see page 52). This contributes to local smog, which, in turn contributes to global warming. Furthermore, people who use cars for transport walk less, which affects their general fitness; and air pollution from cars affects the health of humans, plants and animals.

Hopeful developments

Despite most Sydneysiders' dependence on cars for transport, they rely on their cars half as much as other Australians. 22 per cent of them used public transport to travel to work in 2004, compared to a national average of 10.6 per cent. Sydney has now learned from past mistakes: new homes are planned to be built in locations where people will not have to depend on their cars. This, plus improvements in the public transport system and an increase in cycle use, should decrease Sydneysider's reliance on their cars still further.

▼ The bus network in Sydney is extensive, frequent and good value for money.

Alternatives to the car

Traffic congestion is one reason why fewer people living in central Sydney own a car than in the suburbs (60 per cent as opposed to 85 per cent). Another reason is that parking in central areas is tricky, with only a limited number of spaces.

People in some areas of the city, especially inner areas, have a range of alternatives to the car for getting around.

First and simplest is to walk: central Sydney is very compact, and traffic congestion means that sometimes walking is faster than driving. For longer journeys, cycling is a better option. Cycling and walking have health and environmental benefits, too. Recently, a network of cycle routes have been introduced to make cycling in Sydney safer and more enjoyable.

▲ A monorail system links the Darling Harbour area to the city centre and provides connections to the rail and tram and ferry systems.

Public transport

Central areas of Sydney are well served by public transport, especially an urban rail system that covers the majority of the inner city. The unusual 'double-decker' trains are busy at rush hour in the morning and evening, but they provide a quick, relatively inexpensive way of getting to and from work. There are also regular buses, which have benefited greatly from the introduction of dedicated bus lanes across the city. For moving from one side of the harbour to another, the excellent Sydney Harbour ferries provide a faster and much more enjoyable ride to work than the car. They also provide an alternative way of reaching several of Sydney's harbourside suburbs.

◀ Sydney Harbour ferries docking in Circular Quay, the hub of the city's water transport system.

External transport links

Sydney has the busiest airport in Australia, from which flights leave for domestic as well as international destinations. Sydney has also traditionally been one of Australia's major ports, although use of Sydney Harbour itself as a commercial port has recently declined, with the main port facilities now being located at Botany Bay.

CASE STUDY

Chris Lock, Chief Executive Officer of the Transport Infrastructure Development Corporation

In 2005 Sydney's rail network celebrated 150 years of service to the city, but it is now at a crossroads and needs to be drastically reformed to meet future demands. People regularly complain about the rail service, but as Chris explains: "We are constrained by the geography of the city. We have the ocean to the east, the mountains to the west and national parks to the north and south. This means we have to work with what is there and because much of it is now old this creates problems. We have a project called Clearways that has identified 15 bottlenecks in the system where infrastructure could fail and clog up large parts of the system. More than 1.5 billion Australian dollars (US$1.15 billion) is being spent to remove these bottlenecks. We are also investing in upgraded stations at key points on the network such as here in Parramatta (see image), to provide integrated transfer between the rail and bus networks. Disability access, improved security and new rolling stock are other measures aimed at encouraging people out of their cars and onto the rail network. Ultimately we will need new capacity in the system however. We can expand the network into some of the outer suburbs not currently served and there is provision for that. In the city centre though, it is more complex. Going underground may be a solution, but whatever it is we need to be thinking long term, 2020 and beyond. It is one of the city's biggest challenges."

45

Culture, leisure and tourism

Sydney is a lively, vibrant city with many attractions. Sydneysiders, visitors from elsewhere in Australia and foreign tourists all enjoy the city's theatres, museums, restaurants, beaches and other leisure attractions.

Sydney Opera House

The centrepiece of Sydney's cultural activities is its Opera House. This amazing building stands on the harbour like a series of billowing white sails or giant shells, right in the heart of the City, close to the Royal Botanic Gardens and the Sydney Harbour Bridge.

The design for the Opera House was conceived in the 1950s, and its architect was the Dane Jørn Utzon, whose plans won an international competition to find a designer for the building. The project was planned to cost around US$5 million, and work started in 1959. The Opera House finally cost over US$76 million to build, and wasn't finished until 1973. Utzon had left the project in 1966 after a row with the state government, never to return to Sydney, or indeed Australia. All the drama inspired an opera called 'The Eighth Wonder' about the creation of the building.

Today the Opera House has four main theatres, and people can go there to see opera, classical music, ballet, theatre and films. Popular performances can be difficult to get tickets for, but guided tours of the building are almost as much in demand as the shows themselves. Hundreds of people a day pay to take a tour of the Opera House, making it one of Sydney's most popular tourist attractions, as well as its leading arts venue.

▼ The iconic Sydney Opera House is one of the most recognisable buildings in the world and Sydney's premier tourist attraction.

Galleries and museums

Sydney has some excellent art galleries and museums. The Museum of Sydney is a great place to find out about the early development of the city, and what life was like for the first settlers to live there. The Australian Museum specialises in natural history, with displays about Australia's unique flora and fauna, as well as an area devoted to indigenous Australian culture and beliefs. Nearby, the Art Gallery of New South Wales has displays of European, Asian, Australian and Indigenous Australian art, as well as hosting travelling art exhibitions from around the world.

▲ The Museum of Contemporary Art houses a collection of modern art from Australia and beyond.

Architecture

The modern architecture of the Opera House and the Sydney Harbour Bridge are the most famous sights in the city, but there are some older buildings from the early 1800s that are just as fascinating. The biggest concentration of these is along Macquarie Street in the City: several of these grand buildings were designed by a convict; forger-turned-architect Francis Greenway.

The Sydney Festival

Each January, the city holds the Sydney Festival. This is a month-long celebration of music, art, dance, theatre and film, with lots of events and exhibitions held outdoors in open spaces such as The Domain, the Olympic Park complex and The Rocks, many of them free.

▲▼ Crowds gather to enjoy a free evening of 'Jazz on the Domain' as part of the Sydney Festival.

Sports

Most Australians love sport and Sydney's climate is ideal for outdoor activity. As a result, the pools, rugby pitches and, especially, the beaches are always busy with people enjoying the outdoor life. The sheer variety of sports that Sydneysiders take part in, either as spectators or as participants, can be bewildering to non-Australians.

Among the most popular spectator sports is Rugby League. Sydney is arguably the world's most important rugby-league-playing city: Australia is a dominant force in Rugby League, and Sydney is home to nine of the 15 top-flight teams in Australia. The professional matches attract tens of thousands of spectators every weekend, and the amateur game is also popular.

Sydney is also home to the Sydney Swans Australian Rules Football team. 'Aussie Rules' is one of Australia's most popular sports with almost seven million people going to see live matches in 2005. Aussie Rules is a tough game of kicking and punching or tapping an oval ball. Other top-flight professional sports teams include a rugby union side, a soccer team, two basketball teams, a cricket side and a baseball team.

◄ Sydney residents take part in a 10km run in Centennial Park. Public participation in sporting events is high in Sydney.

The Olympics

In 2000, Sydney played host to the Olympic Games for the first time. Most commentators agreed that it was one of the best Olympics ever held. The friendliness and enthusiasm for sport of Sydneysiders saw smiling faces and packed venues throughout the course of the Games. Sydney was also left with some excellent new sporting facilities, including many at the Sydney Olympic Park. Here there are top-flight facilities for swimming, cycling, athletics and many other sports.

◄ The Telstra Stadium is the main venue in the Olympic Park built for the Sydney 2000 Olympic Games. The Olympics greatly boosted the economy and popularity of the city.

Watersports

Swimming is extremely popular in Sydney, and there are excellent facilities, with pools in most neighbourhoods. People don't only swim in pools, of course. The city's most famous sea-swimming club is the Bondi Icebergs, based at Bondi Beach. To maintain their membership, the Icebergs have to compete in the sea on three Sundays out of every four, even in winter, for five years – hence the chilly name.

Sydney's other favourite watersport is surfing. The city beaches have rideable waves most days, and in winter especially the surf can be enormous. Beaches such as Narrabeen and Cronulla have produced a number of world surfing champions. With all this activity in the sea, people sometimes get into trouble. All the city beaches are looked after by surf lifesavers, most of them volunteers, ready to plunge in and rescue anyone who needs help.

▲ The Bondi Icebergs pool is the most famous of Sydney's many outdoor pools.

▼ The Manly Surf Carnival is one of the biggest beach competitions of the summer. Teams of lifeguards compete against each other and the surf in rowing boats to be the fastest around a course.

Tourism

Tourism plays an extremely important part in Sydney's economy, providing many jobs. Tourists spend their money in obvious areas, such as hotels or visitor attractions like the Harbour Bridge Tour and the Opera House. The money they spend also trickles down to support the city's restaurants, shops, food merchants, taxi drivers and a variety of other businesses.

▼ The Sydney Harbour Bridge climb is one of the city's most popular visitor attractions – as long as you have a head for heights!

▲ There are hundreds of souvenir shops in Sydney to cater for almost every taste.

Over half of international visitors to Australia come to metropolitan Sydney. In addition, the city receives visitors from elsewhere in Australia. In 2004, 2.4 million tourists visited the city, making 5.3 million overnight stays. In the seven years from 2004, the number of overnight stays in the city as a whole is forecast to rise by 4.4 per cent per year, bringing the total number to over seven million by 2011.

At the heart of Sydney's tourist industry is the City of Sydney, which is home to most of the popular visitor attractions. Over 60 per cent of the hotel rooms in the metropolitan region are found within the City of Sydney.

Although overnight visitors play the most important role in the city's tourist economy, because they spend more money, daily visitors also provide employment and help support the infrastructure. 350,000 people a day come into the City to work, but even more, 400,000, come in to be educated, go shopping, eat out or be entertained.

Festivals

Sydney is busy with tourists all year round, but its festivals attract particularly high numbers of visitors. One of these is January's Sydney Festival (see page 47), but probably the most famous Sydney festival is Mardi Gras. This annual celebration of the city's gay and lesbian community, featuring dance, music and the arts is attended by over 450,000 people, and adds roughly US$34 million to the economy.

CASE STUDY

Steven Van Dorp, Mardi Gras organiser

Steven Van Dorp is from Holland, but has been living in Sydney for five months. He came on an internship specifically to help organise the Sydney Gay and Lesbian Mardi Gras festival, a cultural highlight in the Sydney events calendar. "My friend in the UK had been to the Mardi Gras here and told me all about it. It sounded amazing to be part of such a large community event and I knew I wanted to get involved. We have a similar event in Amsterdam called Pride, but it is nowhere near as big as this. My job here is special effects on the parade route and especially the fireworks. This needs a lot of careful planning as the parade is the highlight of the festival for most people. There is still lots to do, but I am looking forward to seeing all the hard work come to fruition. I will make sure I make time to enjoy Mardi Gras too – I have come to the other side of the world for what could be a once in a lifetime opportunity so I'm not going to miss out!"

▼ Crowds enjoy the launch party for Mardi Gras on the steps of the Sydney Opera House.

Sydney's environment

As Sydney has expanded, it has put an increasing strain on its natural resources. The amount of water people use, the waste they create, and the energy they use have all increased. This affects the city's air quality and its biodiversity (the variety of plants and animals that live there). The challenge for Sydney in the future will be to manage its life in a more sustainable way.

Targeting the environment

The New South Wales State Government has targeted five key areas where it hopes to improve Sydney's environmental performance:
• Making water use sustainable, so that water resources do not continue to shrink as they have done in the past.
• Reducing energy demands.
• Improving air quality and reducing air pollution.
• Reducing the amount of waste and dealing with waste in a better way.
• Retaining the city's biodiversity.

▲ Recycling is actively encouraged throughout Sydney in order to reduce the volume of waste disposal.

Air pollution

Air pollution has a serious effect on both the environment and human health. Sydney suffers from serious air pollution, particularly in winter. The decline in heavy industry, once a significant cause of air pollution, has been balanced by the rise in car use. Overall, though, air quality has been improving since the 1980s.

There are two main types of air pollution in the city: photochemical smog and particle pollution.

Smog

Photochemical smog is a whitish haze that forms when sunlight reacts with chemicals in the atmosphere. The chemicals that cause photochemical smog include ozone and nitrogen oxide. Nitrogen oxide is the biggest offender in Sydney, and 80 per cent of it comes from the city's motor vehicles. While the city relies on cars as a main form of transport, smog levels are likely to increase as the population grows. Pollution from cars could even cancel out decreases in pollution from other sources.

▼ The heavy dependence on motor vehicles is a major contributor to air pollution in Sydney.

Particle pollution

Particle pollution is a dark-coloured brown haze. It affects people's health, increasing the likelihood of breathing-related problems such as pneumonia, asthma and bronchitis. About a quarter of Sydney's particle pollution comes from cars. The problem is worse in winter as many Sydneysiders use wood heaters to warm their homes. Wood heater smoke is a major source of air pollution in the city: during winter, on some days it provides three times as much particle pollution as motor vehicles.

Reducing emissions

In 2003, the NSW government introduced new planning regulations called BASIX. The regulations aimed to minimise the environmental impact of new buildings on Sydney's air quality. From July 2004, all new buildings had to produce 25 per cent less greenhouse gas emissions than average New South Wales houses of the same type. From July 2006, the figure rose to 40 per cent less than average. The government calculated that this would reduce carbon emissions by the equivalent of taking half a million cars off the city's roads.

▼ The Watershed Sustainability Resource Centre in Marrickville provides information and workshops for the public about a wide range of environmental and sustainability issues including water use, waste management and recycling, and organic gardening.

Water pollution

Sydney Harbour suffers from pollution from the stormwater drainage system, sewage overflows, run-off from contaminated land and pollution released by vessels using the harbour. In January 2006, a fishing ban – initially for three months – was introduced. This was because high levels of pollution had been carried downstream from chemical and other factories along the Parramatta River. The pollution had caused the build-up of poisonous chemicals in bottom-feeding fish.

Sydney's beaches also suffer from pollution, with pollution from the stormwater and sewage systems being the most serious causes. Since 2000, several deep-ocean outfalls have been built, which pump water-borne waste far out to sea. As a result, the city's beaches and estuaries are cleaner. Another success is the Urban Stormwater Program, which in its first three years prevented roughly 10,800 tonnes of litter and sediment from entering New South Wales waterways.

▼ A sewage outlet pipe runs out to sea at Manly. Any damage to this sewage outlet would cause serious local pollution.

▲ Large ships passing in and out of Sydney Harbour present an environmental risk to the harbour ecosystem. Tugs assist the largest vessels to minimise the risks of any pollution incidents.

Diminishing supplies

Sydneysiders are used to a lifestyle that uses a lot of water. They water their gardens; shower or bathe regularly; and use water in domestic devices like washing machines and dishwashers. But Australia is a dry country, and water resources are not infinite. By 2004, six per cent of the water Sydney used was not being replaced by rainfall or other sources. Sydney was eating into its water reserves at an alarming rate. Under the BASIX regulations (see page 53) new buildings must use 40 per cent less water than the state average, which will help to lessen Sydney's water-supply problems. But it is likely that Sydney's increasing population is going to have to make significant changes if the water supplies are not eventually to run out.

Yvonne Sinanovic, Plant Manager

Yvonne Sinanovic is the Plant Manager at Sydney Water's Rouse Hill Recycled Water Project. This innovative project is located in the north-western suburbs of the city and is part of Sydney Water's plans for managing water resources in the city.

Yvonne explains: "We take normal wastewater, but treat it to a higher than normal standard using micro-filtration and chlorination processes. The end product is recycled water that is perfectly safe to be used for watering private and municipal gardens, cleaning cars, flushing toilets and for some industrial processes. It is not clean enough to drink and people must still be connected to the mains system too. We have been producing recycled water here since August 2001 and there are now over 15,000 properties in the Rouse Hill area connected to the dual pipe system. We hope to add a further 10,000 very soon. The scheme has attracted a great deal of interest because saving water is a big issue in Australia and especially around growing cities like Sydney. In the households connected to this system, drinking water consumption has fallen by around 35 per cent, a major contribution to making water use more sustainable."

The Sydney of tomorrow

What kind of city is Sydney likely to become in the future? The kind of city it will be when its children reach adulthood depends on a number of key issues, not all of them within the control of Sydney's governing bodies. Some of the things that will affect the Sydney of tomorrow are linked to events elsewhere. These include Australian national politics, globalisation of the world economy and changes in the world's environment (particularly global warming).

Multiculturalism

One key challenge for Sydney is going to be how it deals with minority groups who make up an increasing proportion of the city's people. Most Sydneysiders are white and of European descent, and recent immigrants have been integrated into society with varying degrees of success. One possible problem is the potential for conflict between parts of Sydney's Muslim community and other citizens. Clashes have already occurred between young Australian Muslim men, mainly from Lebanese families, and other young Australians. Helping these two communities to live peacefully is important to Sydney's future. A second challenge is to make sure that Sydney's Indigenous Australians begin to enjoy the same economic, healthcare, educational and housing status as their non-indigenous fellow citizens. Initiatives like 'Lights Camera Action!' and the city's redevelopment plans for public spaces in areas such as Redfern (see pages 22-23) are part of this process.

▼ This memorial on Coogee Beach is for the 89 Australian tourists who were killed in the Bali bomb attack in October 2002.

The environment

Sydney's growing population means that the city's environment could change for the worse in the future. The clean air, the beaches, the green spaces, plants and animals of the city are all reasons why people want to live there. If air and water pollution grow at the same speed as the population, all could suffer. Fortunately, the city has started to take measures aimed at reducing car dependence, keeping the waters clean and improving air quality.

Over-use of water is another challenge, since water is a basic requirement of human life. Again, though, action is being taken to improve the situation, through the city's insistence that new housing developments must use less water, more efficiently than in the past.

▼ Sydney is located within some of Australia's most scenic landscapes such as here in Royal National Park. Efforts must be made now to make sure these landscapes are preserved for future generations.

The economy

Sydney's economy has moved from being based around industry and shipping, to being shaped around services such as banking and tourism. This leaves it less vulnerable than in the past to changes in the global price of, for example, coal or steel. However, industries such as banking and tourism are becoming increasingly globalised, which can make them vulnerable to global economic trends and world events. Sydney's economy, like that of all wealthy nations, will also have to deal with increasing challenges from emerging developing countries like China and India.

Despite these challenges, Sydney remains one of the world's most significant cities, and continues to grow quickly. The city's policies of trying to encourage development in sustainable communities, each with its own shops, leisure facilities and public transport links, while also safeguarding the environment for the future, should ensure that it remains a global city far into the twenty-first century.

Glossary

Asia-Pacific Rim The countries and landmasses surrounding the Pacific Ocean, including Hong Kong, South Korea, Singapore, Taiwan, China, Malaysia, Indonesia, the Philippines, New Zealand, and Australia.

Congestion Overcrowding that makes movement slow or difficult. If roads are congested, it means there are so many vehicles that they cannot move freely, resulting in traffic jams and hold-ups.

Conscription The requirement for people, usually at a particular age such as 18 or 21, to serve their country. People are normally conscripted into the armed forces, but sometimes are able to work in the health service or some other organisation that benefits the public.

Detached Not touching anything else. A detached house, for example, is one that doesn't touch any other houses and has space all around it.

Federal A form of government where some powers belong to the central government, while other powers belong to the states or regions. Australia and the USA both have a federal system of government.

Global warming A steady rise in the Earth's average temperature, which most scientists agree is a result of air pollution caused by human activities.

Great Depression A period of time during the 1930s when the world's trade slowed down and businesses found it hard to make money. As a result, work was hard to find, unemployment was high, and many people struggled to keep a home and enough food on the table.

Head of state The chief representative of a country. The head of state may also be the head of the government, as with the US president, or not, as with the Queen in Australia and Britain.

Industrial Revolution A period that began during the eighteenth century, when the economy in Britain, then the USA and parts of Europe, began to change from being based on agriculture to being based on industry.

Infant mortality The number of children who die before they are one year old. Infant mortality rates are often used as a measure of how good health care is.

Infrastructure Roads, railways, other transport systems, energy and water supply systems, schools and the other facilities that are necessary for a developed area to continue to work.

Obesity The condition of being so overweight that it is likely to harm one's health.

Particle pollution A form of air pollution where tiny bits, or particles, of solid material are released into the air.

Photochemical smog A whitish-coloured haze that forms when sunlight reacts with chemicals.

Prospecting Searching for precious metals, in particular gold or gemstones.

Referendum A vote by a group of people on a specific issue or issues, such as a change in the way their country is governed.

Stormwater Rainwater that enters the drainage system. In Sydney, rainwater runs off the streets and into the drainage system, then straight into the harbour or sea. On the way it collects cigarette butts, discarded packaging and other waste.

Sustainable Using natural resources without upsetting the natural balance of an area, meaning that the resources will still be there for people to use in the future.

Symbol Something that stands for or represents something else.

Vocational Linked to a particular job or career.

Further information

Books to read
Non-fiction

Countries of the World: Australia Robert Prosser (Evans Brothers, 2004)

A general book about Australia that also contains information about Sydney, along with facts and figures, useful maps and interesting photos.

The Danger Zone: Avoid Being A Convict In Australia! Meredith Costain (Book House, 2005)

A light-hearted look at some of the problems faced by people transported to Australia as a punishment.

Gold! The Fascinating Story of Gold in Australia John Nicolson (Allen and Unwin, 1994)

An old book now, but still available, *Gold!* tells you everything you could want to know about gold mining in Australia, especially the Gold Rush.

Take Care! Poisonous Australian Animals Struan Sutherland and Susie Kennewell (Hyland House, 2005)

An Australia-wide survey of some of the animals to avoid if you ever visit Sydney!

The New Dinkum Aussie Dictionary by R Beckett (New Holland Australia, 2000) and *Culture Shock! Australia: A Guide To Customs And Etiquette* by Ilsa Sharp (Kuperard, 1992)

These books will furnish you with an understanding of Australian-English and Australian manners.

Fiction

Transported: The Diary of Elizabeth Harvey, Australia, 1790 Goldie Alexander (Scholastic, 2002)

The story of a young woman who is transported to Australia from England.

Useful websites

Websites: general

http://ceroi.net/cle/

This site for a City Lifestyle Explorer allows you to discover how your actions as a city dweller have an impact on the city's environment.

Websites: Sydney

The New South Wales Government and the City of Sydney both have excellent websites with a wealth of up-to-date information about Sydney and its people and environment.

http://www.cityofsydney.nsw.gov.au/

This excellent site is a good starting point for anyone interested in the history, people and environment of Sydney's inner and most important area, the City of Sydney.

http://www.metrostrategy.nsw.gov.au/

The New South Wales government site on Sydney has sections on urban growth, housing, the economy, employment, natural resources, the city's green spaces, transport and infrastructure.

http://en.wikipedia.org/wiki/Sydney

The online encyclopedia has general information about Sydney, plus some useful links to allow you to find out more information.

http://www.dreamtime.net.au/

This site, managed by the Australian Museum, provides information about Indigenous Australians.

Index

Aborigines 12, 22
Adelaide 24
airports 45
architecture 47
Art Gallery of New South
    Wales 47
Asia-Pacific Rim 18
Aussie Rules 48
Australia 9, 11-12, 14, 16, 18,
    20, 22, 24, 29-33, 35-36,
    39, 43, 45-46, 48, 50, 54-57
Australian Catholic
    University 30
Australian Museum 14, 47

Bali bomb attacks 56
BASIX 53-54
beaches 11, 20, 24-25, 54
biodiversity 24, 52
Blue Mountains 11, 28
Bondi Beach 25, 49
Bondi Icebergs 49
Botany Bay 45
Britain 11, 14, 16-17, 20
bus network 43, 44

Cabramatta 21
Cadman's Cottage 12
Carlton and United Brewery
    35-36, 40
cars 42-44
Case Studies 17, 19, 24, 29,
    31, 33-34, 37, 39, 41, 45,
    51, 55
Centennial Park 24, 48
Central Business District
    (CBD) 9-10, 32, 35
Central Station 40
Chinatown 10, 18, 21
Chinese community 14, 21
Chinese Garden of
    Friendship 36-37
Chippendale 35
Circular Quay 12, 44
citizenship 9, 17-19, 21-23,
    56
city government 23, 35, 40
city living 18, 24

city management 38
City of Sydney 10-11, 15, 18,
    21, 24-26, 28, 32, 35, 38,
    39, 40, 46, 50
climate 24-25, 48
Cockle Bay 36
colony 12
Commonwealth
    Parliamentary Debates 16
community groups 40
congestion 42, 43-44
convicts 12
Coogee Beach 56
crime 25
Cronulla 49
cultural identity 17-21
culture 9, 13, 16-17, 46
cycling 44

Darling Harbour 10, 19, 36,
    37, 44
Darlinghurst 21
Deakin, Alfred 16
deep-ocean outfalls 54
didgeridoos 13
diversity 20
docks 36
Domain, the 47
Dutch auction 29

economic zones 34
economy 9-10, 15, 32, 34,
    36, 50-51, 56-57
education 9, 13, 23, 30-31,
    38, 50, 56
Eighth Wonder, the 46
elections 40
emissions 53
employment 10, 15, 22-23,
    33-34, 50
energy 52
England 12-13, 17
environment 36, 44, 52-53,
    56-57
Eora people 13
ethnic cultures 23
ethnic origins 16
ethnic tensions 20

Europe 12, 16-17, 20

farmland 28,
federal government 31, 38
ferries 44
festivals 51
financial services 10, 33
First Fleet 12, 37
fish market 28-29
future 26, 56-57

galleries 47
gangs 25
gay and lesbian community
    51
General Post Office (GPO)
    14
Glebe 15
global city 9, 11, 39
global warming 43, 56
globalisation 9, 34, 56-57
gold rush 14
Great Depression, the 15
green spaces 19, 24, 27
Green Square 35

harbour 11, 13-14, 26, 44, 54
Harbour Bridge Tour 50
health 13, 22, 28, 38, 43-44,
    52-53
health care 9, 23, 31, 33, 56
history 12
hospitals 31
housing 19-24, 26-28, 38, 43
Hyde Park 24

immigrants 11, 14, 16-21, 31,
    56
Indigenous Australians 12-
    13, 21-23, 47, 56
Industrial Revolution 14
industries 10, 32-34
infant mortality 22
infrastructure 38, 45, 50

Keating, Paul 18
King's School 30

law enforcement 38
leisure 46, 57
life expectancy 13, 22
lifesavers 49
Lights Camera Action! 23, 56
local councils 39
local government 11, 38, 40

Macquarie Bank 33
Macquarie Street 47
Manly 11
Manly Surf Carnival 49, 54
manufacturing industry 32-34
Mardi Gras 51
market gardens 28
Marrickville 21, 40, 53
mayor 39
Medicare 31
Melbourne 24
metropolitan area 11, 18, 25-26, 32, 39, 40, 50
Military Road 42
multiculturalism 9, 56
Museum of Contemporary Art 47
Museum of Sydney 47
museums 14, 36, 47

Narrabeen 49
National Maritime Museum 36
New South Wales 9, 12, 14, 30-31, 39, 52-54

obesity 28
Olympic Games 41, 48
Olympic Park 47-48
Opera House 9, 10, 46, 50-51
overcrowded housing 22

parking 44
Parramatta 45
Parramatta River 54
Parramatta Road 42

people 11, 16, 20, 25
Perth 24
police 22
political outlook 18
pollution 8, 27, 43, 52, 53, 57
population 8-9, 11, 14-15, 18-19, 21, 26-27, 42, 54, 57
Port Botany 35
port of Sydney 14-15, 34, 45
poverty 25
prospecting 14
public buildings 14
Pyrmont 15

Queen Victoria Building 28

railways 9, 36, 42, 44, 45
Reclaim the Beach 20
recycling 9, 52, 53, 55
Redfern 15, 22-23, 56
referendum 18
regeneration 15, 27, 35-37, 56
Royal Botanic Gardens 9, 10, 24, 46
Royal National Park 57

schools 30
sealing 14
Second World War 16
settlements 11-12
settlers 13
sewage management 54
shipping 36, 57
shopping 28, 36-37, 50, 57
smog 43, 52
sports 48-49
standard of living 22, 24-25
state government 30-31, 38, 46
street market 37
suburbs 11, 15, 19-21, 24, 26, 28, 42, 44-45
subways 9
Summer Hill 26, 42
Surry Hills 17, 40
sustainability 9, 26-27, 35-36, 43-45, 52-55, 57

Sydney Aquarium 36, 37
Sydney Convention Centre 36
Sydney Cove 12
Sydney Festival 47, 51
Sydney Harbour 13, 45, 54
Sydney Harbour Bridge 15, 32, 46-47, 50
Sydney Harbour Foreshore Authority 36, 37
Sydneysiders 16, 19-20, 24, 28, 31, 37, 40, 43, 46, 48, 53-54, 56

Taronga Zoo 41
telecommunications 10
Telstra Stadium 48
'terra nullius' 12
terrorists 20
The Rocks 10, 28, 36, 37, 47
tourism 10, 13, 25, 33, 37, 46, 50-51, 57
Town Hall 14, 38
transport 9, 28, 33, 38, 42, 44-45, 52, 57

unemployment 13
universities 30-31
University of New South Wales 30
University of Sydney 30
University of Technology 30-31
University of Western Sydney 30
Urban Stormwater Program 54
urbanisation 8-9, 19, 39, 42, 52

Victoria Road 42
Vietnam 17
Vietnamese community 21

waste management 9, 52, 54, 55